The Ramayana School

Knowledge Partner

Indian Knowledge System (IKS) Series

OCCAM

Masterclass with Yogi Adityanath on Kumbh Mela

Shantanu Gupta

Layout and typsetting: Anand Upadhyay and Pallavi Saxena

ISBN: 978-93-65474-29-9

First published in India 2025
This edition published 2025

Published by
BluOne Ink Pvt. Ltd
A-76, 2nd Floor, Sector 136, Noida
Uttar Pradesh 201305

Website: www.bluone.ink
Email: publisher@bluone.ink

Printed and bound in India at Nutech Print Services - India

Kali and Occam are imprints of BluOne Ink

From the Author's Desk

Namaste parents and children!

Celebrated since time immemorial, Kumbh Mela is a grand and deeply significant gathering of people belonging to the Hindu faith. Its origins are rooted in ancient Puranic stories, and its observance is shaped by specific astrological alignments, a rich history of celebrations, and an evolving tradition over the years. Recognized by UNESCO as an intangible cultural heritage, Kumbh Mela holds a special place in the cultural and spiritual fabric of India.

This book is my honest attempt to bring the essence, stories, concepts, and history of the Kumbh Mela to every Sanatani family and every child across the globe.

I am deeply grateful to my friends and colleagues who made this book possible. Anand Upadhyay and Pallavi Saxena assisted with the book's design, while my wife, Swetha Rao Duggu, lent her expertise in editing. My children, Abhiram and Tara, reviewed the book with the fresh perspective of young readers, ensuring it resonates with children.

Masterclass with Yogi Adityanath on Kumbh Mela is part of the Indian Knowledge System (IKS) Series of books I have written and plan to continue writing. These books include critical thinking exercises, visual and art-based activities, vocabulary-building tasks, and reflective puzzles. With the National Education Policy (NEP) by the Government of India emphasizing the Indian knowledge system, this book is a humble contribution to that vision.

Jai Shri Ram!

MASTERCLASS
on KUMBH
Children, this is Yogi Adityanath ji, the chief minister of Uttar Pradesh. We are glad that he is in our midst today.
I know you all have many questions about Kumbh Mela. Why don't you direct them to him.
My question is very basic. What is Kumbh, Yogi ji?

MASTERCLASS
on KUMBH
The word "kumbh" is an earthen pot, like the matka you use in your house to keep water.

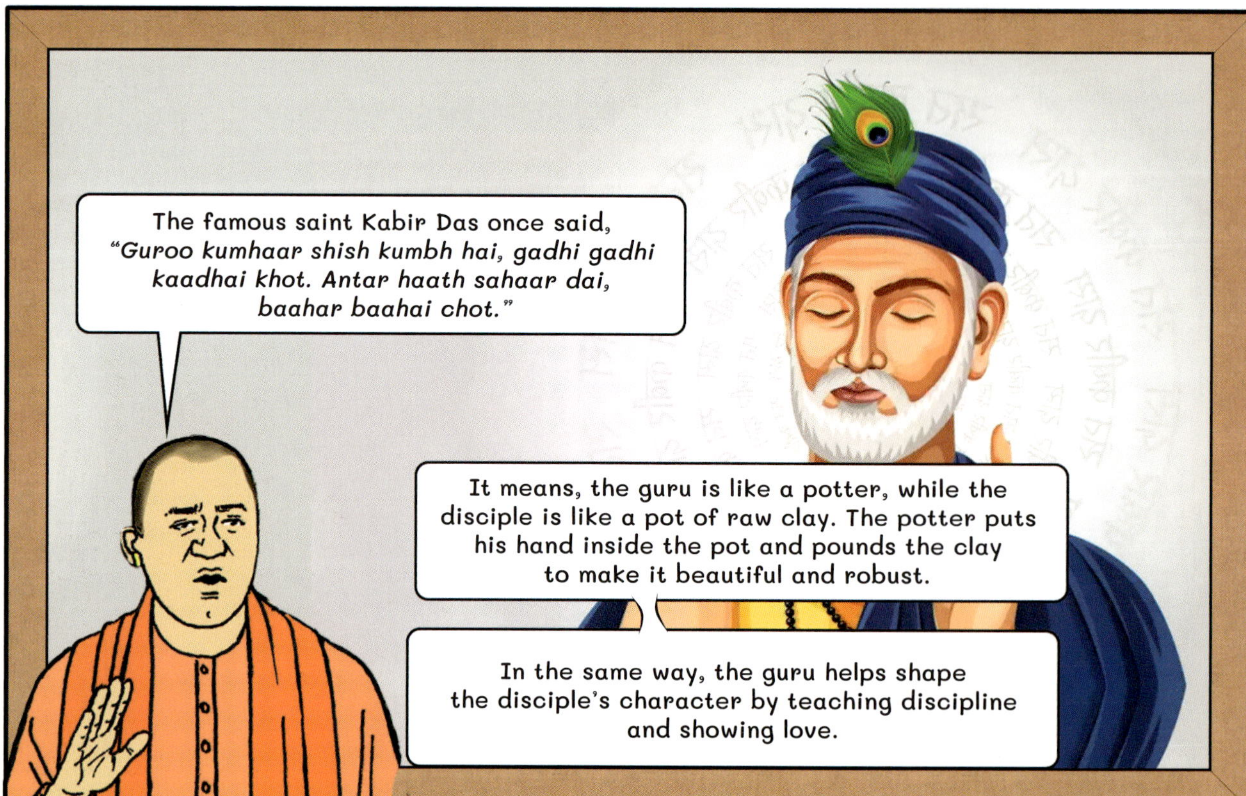
The famous saint Kabir Das once said, *"Guroo kumhaar shish kumbh hai, gadhi gadhi kaadhai khot. Antar haath sahaar dai, baahar baahai chot."*
It means, the guru is like a potter, while the disciple is like a pot of raw clay. The potter puts his hand inside the pot and pounds the clay to make it beautiful and robust.
In the same way, the guru helps shape the disciple's character by teaching discipline and showing love.

MESH
MEEN
KUMBH
MAKAR
DHANU
VRISHCHIK
TULA
KANYA
SIMHA
KARK
MITHUN
VRISHABH
Kumbha is also a zodiac sign or a rashi. It stands for the zodiac sign Aquarius.

Then what is Kumbh Mela Yogi ji? A mela where we get a lot of matkas?

No, no! Kumbh Mela is a very important and grand gathering of people of Hindu faith, celebrated since time immemorial. In fact, Kumbh Mela is the largest spiritual gathering in the world.
Kumbh Mela is rooted in a fascinating Puranic story that explains its origins. It's celebrated at specific locations, guided by astrology, and has a rich history of gatherings. Over the years, Kumbh Mela has evolved in many ways, adding layers of tradition, culture, and meaning to its legacy. There's so much to explore! What exactly do you want to know?

MASTERCLASS
I want to know the story of Kumbh Mela? Why and how was it started?
Hmmm, let me explain this in detail then.
Rawat ji, shift my afternoon meetings to evening and let's record this, so that it can be shared with other children too.
What's your name beta?
Yogi ji, my name is Ganga.
To understand Kumbh Mela, we have to go back to the Puranic times, to the story of Samudra Manthan—or the great churning of the ocean.

Who churned the sea and why did they do it, Yogi ji?

Long ago, Rishi Durvasa cursed Indra and the devas to lose their power after Indra placed a garland offered by the rishi on his elephant Airavata.

Airavata, irritated by the scent of the garland, picked it with his trunk and threw it on the ground. Rishi Durvasa got furious and cursed Indra and the devas to lose their kingdom, power, and glory.

Oh! What happened then, Yogi ji?
Then Indra's mighty vahana Airavata instantly went into oblivion.
Lakshmi, the goddess of fortune, could no longer stay in the same realm as the devas, and parted ways with Bhagwan Vishnu. She made the depths of Kshir Sagar her new home.
And due to Lakshmi's absence in Devlok, the devas lost all their wealth and riches.
The luminous Chandra, who adorned Shiva's matted hair, disappeared too.

What happened to the devas then? Did they ever regain their power and wealth?

Not so easily. The asuras saw this opportunity and attacked the devas. Robbed of their power, the devas were soon defeated by the asuras in battle.

Oh! And then?

The defeated devas approached Lord Vishnu for a solution, who advised them to churn Kshir Sagar, to obtain amrit. Amrit or the nectar of immortality would help the devas regain their powers.

And that's how came the idea of Samudra Manthan, or the great churning of the ocean.

Churning an ocean sounds very tough, Yogi ji? Who all did it?
Very sharp observation. It was indeed tough. Bhagwan Vishnu advised the devas to somehow convince and involve asuras too in the massive churning exercise.
Did the asuras agree to join?
Yes, they did join. The asuras offered to assist their half-brothers, the devas, since they too wanted immortality and invincible powers by consuming amrit.

But Yogi ji, to churn the ocean, don't we need a big churning rod, a base, and a large rope to rotate the churning rod?
Very true and correct. We need all of that.
Mount Mandara was used as the churning rod, kept afloat by Kurma, Vishnu's turtle avatar. The naga king, Vasuki, whom Shiva wears as a garland, became the churning rope.
In fact, Bhagwan Vishnu took his second avatar, that is Kurma Avatar, especially for this gigantic task.

What happened after the churning of the ocean, Yogi ji?
Several precious items, called ratnas, emerged from the churning of the ocean.
Who took these ratnas home?
First, let us learn what came out of the churning. First came Halahal or Kalakoot, a deadly poison, and obviously there were no takers for it.
Halahal poison was strong enough to kill all beings from all three realms. None amongst the armies of asuras and devas stepped in to stop the poison from spreading into the universe as they feared the poison would destroy them too.

Oh, did the Halahal destroy life in the universe then, Yogi ji?
It would have, but Lord Shiva descended from Mount Kailash to consume the poison.
Oh! Shiva consumed the deadly poison! What happened to Shiva then?
Everyone has the same concern for Shiva. But, it was Goddess Parvati who used her powers to stop the Halahal in Shiva's throat, and as a result, his throat turned blue.
I think that's why we also call Shiva as Neelkanth, meaning blue-throated.
Absolutely correct.

Another ratna that emerged from the churning was Goddess Lakshmi herself—the goddess of wealth, prosperity, and fortune. After a long separation, the goddess was finally reunited with Bhagwan Vishnu.
Oh ya! She went away after Rishi Durvasa's curse.
कौस्तुभ.
लक्ष्मी.
रंभा.
Exactly, and with her, the wealth and prosperity of the devas returned, giving devaloka its earlier splendour.
Along with Lakshmi also came apsaras, like Rambha, Menaka, Punjisthala, and others, who chose the Gandharvas as their companions.
Then came Varuni, the goddess of sura, or wine, who was chosen by the asuras because of the toxic taste and bad effect of sura on the mind.

Yogi ji, I heard that some divine animals also came out of the churning?
Yes, three types of supernatural animals appeared.
Kamadhenu or Surabhi, the wish-granting cow, which was taken by Brahma and given to the sages so that the ghee from her milk could be used for yajnas and other rituals. Today, in UP, we have an Uttar Pradesh Kamdhenu Dairy Scheme to help dairy farmers in the state.
Then came Indra's Airavata elephant, the same one that had gone away earlier due to Rishi Durvasa's curse.
Then came Uchhaishravas, the divine seven-headed horse. It was also taken by Indra.

Then the Moon god, Chandra, appeared as one of the precious ratnas.
Let me take you back in time. Chandra's father-in-law, Prajapati Daksha, once cursed him for not being a good husband to his daughters. Because of the curse, Chandra lost his powers, and his body began to wither.

Oh, is it?
When Chandra emerged from the grand churning, Shiva came to the deity's rescue and wore him as an ornament in his hair to neutralize the curse.

Then came a divine flowering tree called parijat from the depths of the ocean.
Yogi ji, we call parijat, "Raat Ki Rani" in our village, as these flowers release a beautiful scent at night.
Yes, you are right Ganga. In fact, Indra took this beautiful flowering tree and planted it in the gardens of devaloka.
Yugas later, Krishna and Indra dueled over the tree, and Krishna brought the tree bearing these white-scented flowers to prithviloka.
According to legend, it is forbidden to pluck its flowers. Only those that have fallen should be used for worship.

So, did any more ratnas emerge from Samudra Manthan?
Yes, next came Vishnu's Sharanga bow, the Panchajanya conch, and Kaustubh Mani.
What are these ratnas exactly?
The Sharanga bow was one of the two divine bows crafted by Vishwakarma, the architect of the gods. Vishnu used this bow in his Parshurama, Rama, and Krishna avatars.
Vishnu's conch, Panchajanya, is a symbolic way of portraying his role as the preserver of the universe. Remember, in the Mahabharata war, Krishna blew his Panchajanya conch to signal the start of the battle of Kurukshetra and at the end to symbolize the victory of dharma.
Kaustubh Mani is a sacred precious gemstone that is embedded in the necklace worn by Vishnu. The gemstone is said to be as beautiful as an exotic lotus and as radiant as the Sun.

But Yogi ji, the devas performed the Samudra Manthan to obtain amrit? What happened to that?
Ah! Good that you remember this.
Towards the end, Dhanvantri, the physician of the gods, appeared from the turbulent ocean carrying the pot of amrit.
Yogi ji, tell us more about Dhanvantri.
Dhanvantri was responsible for teaching the ancient knowledge of medical science, Ayurveda, to the mortals.
Brahma created Ayurveda before he created mankind, but the vast knowledge of medical science was difficult for mortals to understand. So, Dhanvantri split the original text into eight divisions and taught his disciples.

So, finally, the devas got the amrit for which they had performed Samudra Manthan?
No, no, Ganga, it was not that simple. As soon as Dhanvantri appeared with the pot of amrit, the asuras snatched the pot and tried to consume all of it!
OMG! Then?
Beta, it was Bhagwan Vishnu's plan. How could he allow the Samudra Manthan to go in vain?

Vishnu took the form of the enchanting Mohini, using her charm to lure the asuras out of hiding and seizing the opportunity to retrieve the pot of amrit for the devas!

As the devas began consuming the amrit to regain their divine strength, an asura named Rahuketu disguised himself as a deva and managed to taste the nectar.

However, just as he poured the amrit into his mouth, his deception was discovered. Vishnu immediately hurled the Sudarshan Chakra, beheading Rahuketu. By then, the amrit had already reached his throat. Separated from his body, Rahuketu's head and torso were flung to the opposite ends of the universe, where they became Rahu and Ketu.

In this fierce tussle for the pot, drops of amrit fell at four places: Haridwar, Prayag (Prayagraj), Trimbak (Nashik), and Ujjain. Kumbh Mela is celebrated at these four holy places.

And why do people take bath at Kumbh Mela?

The nectar fell into different rivers at these four sacred pilgrimage sites: at the confluence of the Ganges, Yamuna, and Saraswati rivers in Prayagraj; the Ganges in Haridwar; the Godavari in Nashik; and the Shipra in Ujjain.
So, during Kumbh Mela, people take holy dips in the rivers at these sites.

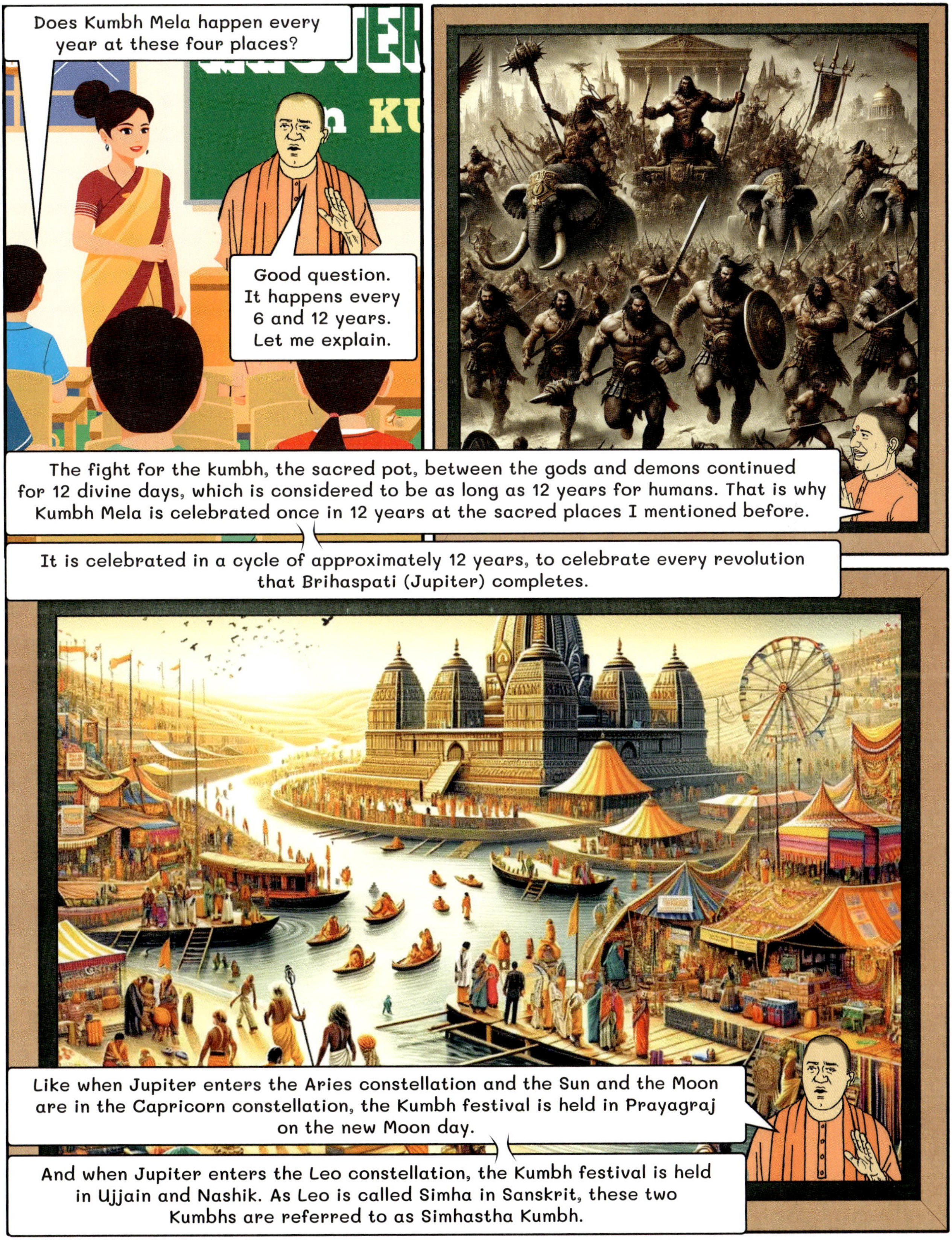
Does Kumbh Mela happen every year at these four places?
Good question. It happens every 6 and 12 years. Let me explain.
The fight for the kumbh, the sacred pot, between the gods and demons continued for 12 divine days, which is considered to be as long as 12 years for humans. That is why Kumbh Mela is celebrated once in 12 years at the sacred places I mentioned before.
It is celebrated in a cycle of approximately 12 years, to celebrate every revolution that Brihaspati (Jupiter) completes.
Like when Jupiter enters the Aries constellation and the Sun and the Moon are in the Capricorn constellation, the Kumbh festival is held in Prayagraj on the new Moon day.
And when Jupiter enters the Leo constellation, the Kumbh festival is held in Ujjain and Nashik. As Leo is called Simha in Sanskrit, these two Kumbhs are referred to as Simhastha Kumbh.

And one more thing: remember that Kumbh Mela (earlier called Ardh Kumbh) is held every 6 years in Haridwar and Prayagraj, while the Maha Kumbh Mela (earlier called Kumbh Mela) takes place every 12 years at 4 places (Parayagraj, Haridwar, Ujjain, and Nashik) based on planetary movements.

Yogi ji, in which months of the year does Kumbh Mela happen at these places?
In Prayagraj, it happens in the Magha month (January—February).
In Haridwar, it happens in the Chaitra month (March—April).
In Nashik, it happens in the Bhadrapada month (August—September).
In Ujjain, it happens in the Vaisakha month (April—May).

Yogi ji, since when are we celebrating Kumbh Mela?
Hmm, very good question again. I am so glad that children of Uttar Pradesh are taking so much interest in Kumbh Mela.
There is a mention of Kumbh and the bathing ritual associated with it in the Rig Veda (verse 10.89.7). It speaks of the benefits of bathing at the "sangam" in Prayag during this period to eliminate negative influences and rejuvenate the mind and soul.
Prayers for the Kumbh are also expressed in Atharva Veda and Yajur Veda.
Historic evidence points towards the rule of King Harshvardhana (AD 590-647) as the time when Kumbh Mela got widespread recognition across geographies.

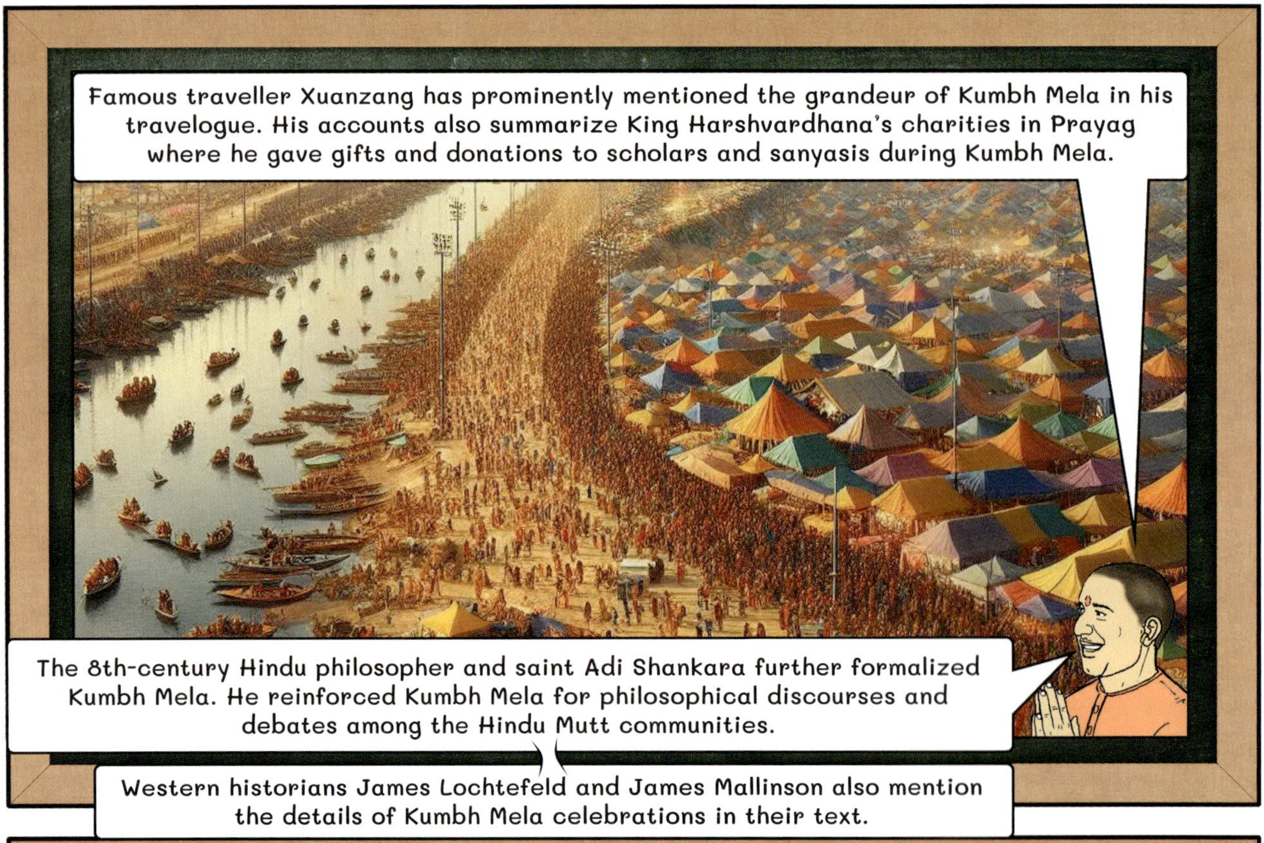
Famous traveller Xuanzang has prominently mentioned the grandeur of Kumbh Mela in his travelogue. His accounts also summarize King Harshvardhana's charities in Prayag where he gave gifts and donations to scholars and sanyasis during Kumbh Mela.
The 8th-century Hindu philosopher and saint Adi Shankara further formalized Kumbh Mela. He reinforced Kumbh Mela for philosophical discourses and debates among the Hindu Mutt communities.
Western historians James Lochtefeld and James Mallinson also mention the details of Kumbh Mela celebrations in their text.

Acharya Tulsidas describes Prayag as the "king of pilgrimages" in the Ayodhya Kanda of *Ramcharitmanas*.
Even Islamic texts like *Ain-i-Akbari* and *Tabaqat-i-Akbari* mention Kumbh Mela.

Yogi ji, who all attend Kumbh Mela? Is it only for sanyasis?
Sanyasis and grhasthas (householders) both join in large numbers in Kumbh Melas. Many sadhus participate as members of their akharas. But even those who do not belong to any of the dozen-plus akharas join in!

Akharas? Oh, so there are wrestling matches also at Kumbh Mela?
No beta. On hearing the word "akhara", wrestling comes to mind. But here, the word "akhara" means "akhand", whose literal meaning is indivisible. Adi Guru Shankaracharya attempted to unite organizations of ascetics to protect the Sanatan way of life, and that is how different akharas were formed.

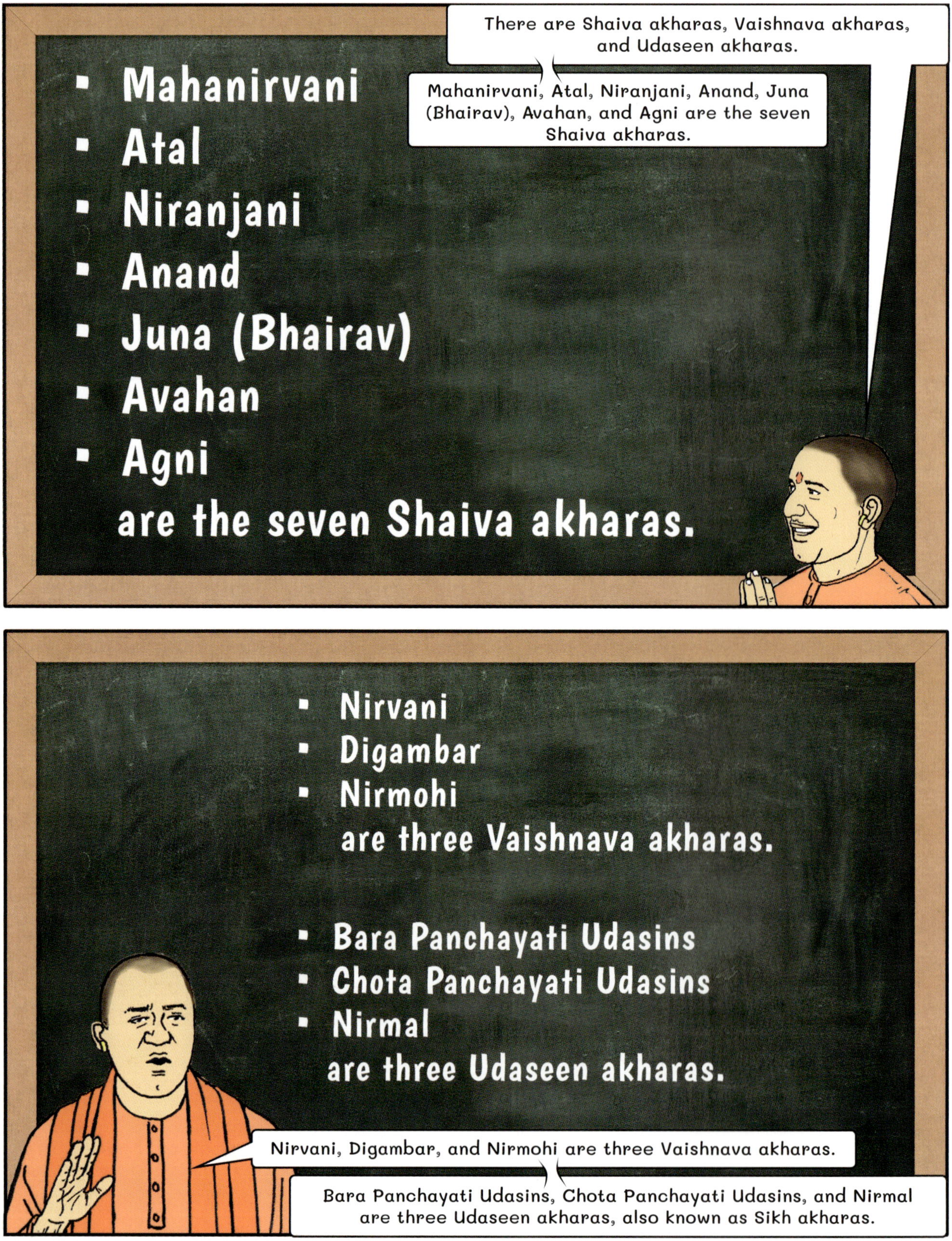
There are Shaiva akharas, Vaishnava akharas, and Udaseen akharas.
Mahanirvani, Atal, Niranjani, Anand, Juna (Bhairav), Avahan, and Agni are the seven Shaiva akharas.
▪ Mahanirvani
▪ Atal
▪ Niranjani
▪ Anand
▪ Juna (Bhairav)
▪ Avahan
▪ Agni
are the seven Shaiva akharas.
▪ Nirvani
▪ Digambar
▪ Nirmohi
are three Vaishnava akharas.
▪ Bara Panchayati Udasins
▪ Chota Panchayati Udasins
▪ Nirmal
are three Udaseen akharas.
Nirvani, Digambar, and Nirmohi are three Vaishnava akharas.
Bara Panchayati Udasins, Chota Panchayati Udasins, and Nirmal are three Udaseen akharas, also known as Sikh akharas.

Juna akhara is the largest among these akharas, closely followed by Niranjani and Mahanirvani akharas.

Mahamandaleshwaras lead their respective akharas, and they are the only ones authorized to share the guru mantra to the newly inducted saints.
Kids, you should observe the procession of akharas in Kumbh Mela during the Peshvai and Shahi Snans. It's a spectacle in itself!

Yogi ji, what happens during these processions?

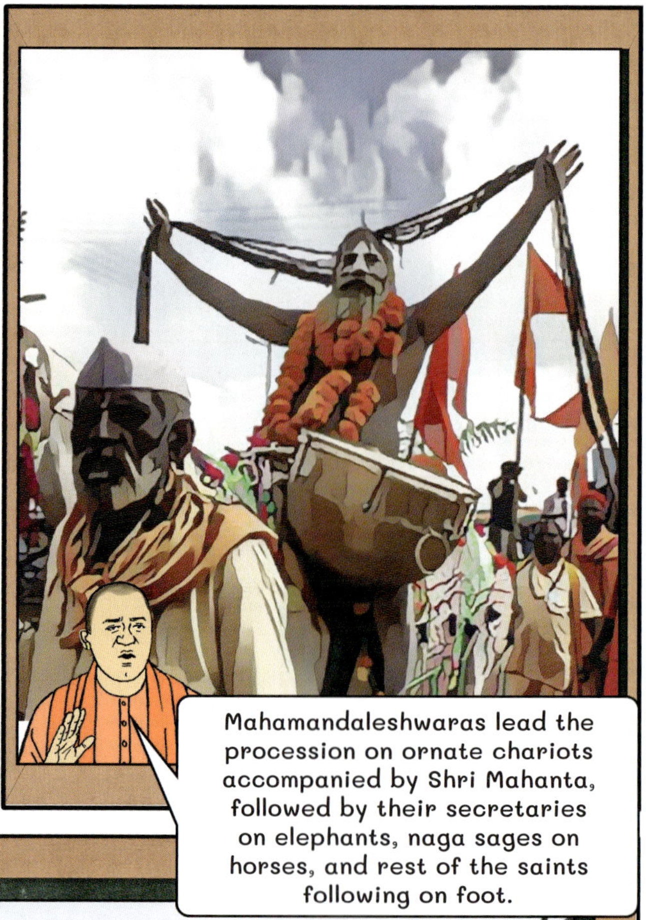
Mahamandaleshwaras lead the procession on ornate chariots accompanied by Shri Mahanta, followed by their secretaries on elephants, naga sages on horses, and rest of the saints following on foot.

Akharas display their royal glory by displaying their skills using traditional weapons along with all the paraphernalia during the procession.

Yogi ji, what do householders do at Kumbh Mela?
Many devotees come to take a dip at the holy river at the mela site.
For example, Paush Purnima, Makar Sankranti, Mauni Amavasya, Basant Panchami, Maghi Purnima, and Maha Shivratri are important dates for the Shahi Snan at the Prayag Kumbh. Along with sadhus, crores of devotees also take a dip at the sangam on these occasions.
Crores of people in a day? But Yogi ji, that's more than the total population of Prayagraj! How is that possible?
We make it possible. Like during the 2019 Prayag Ardh Kumbh, 5 crore people took a dip on Mauni Amavasya day. For Kumbh, we create a separate city called Kumbh Mela City along the banks of the holy river.

Yogi ji, what exactly is kalpvas? In the 2019 Prayag Kumbh, some families from my neighbourhood went for kalpvas.
Many devotees live by the banks of the river for a month or more following 21 strict guidelines during Kumbh. That's called kalpvas. And people practising it are called kalpvasis.
21 guidelines? That's a lot. What kind of guidelines Yogi ji?
According to Maharishi Dhatatreya, anyone observing a 30—45 days kalpvas must observe the following 21 guidelines.
(1) Speak only truth, (2) observe non-violence, (3) control all senses, (4) have mercy on all living beings, (5) follow Brahmacharya, (6) give up all forms of addiction, (7) wake up 1 hr 36 minutes before sunrise, which is the Brahm Muhrat.

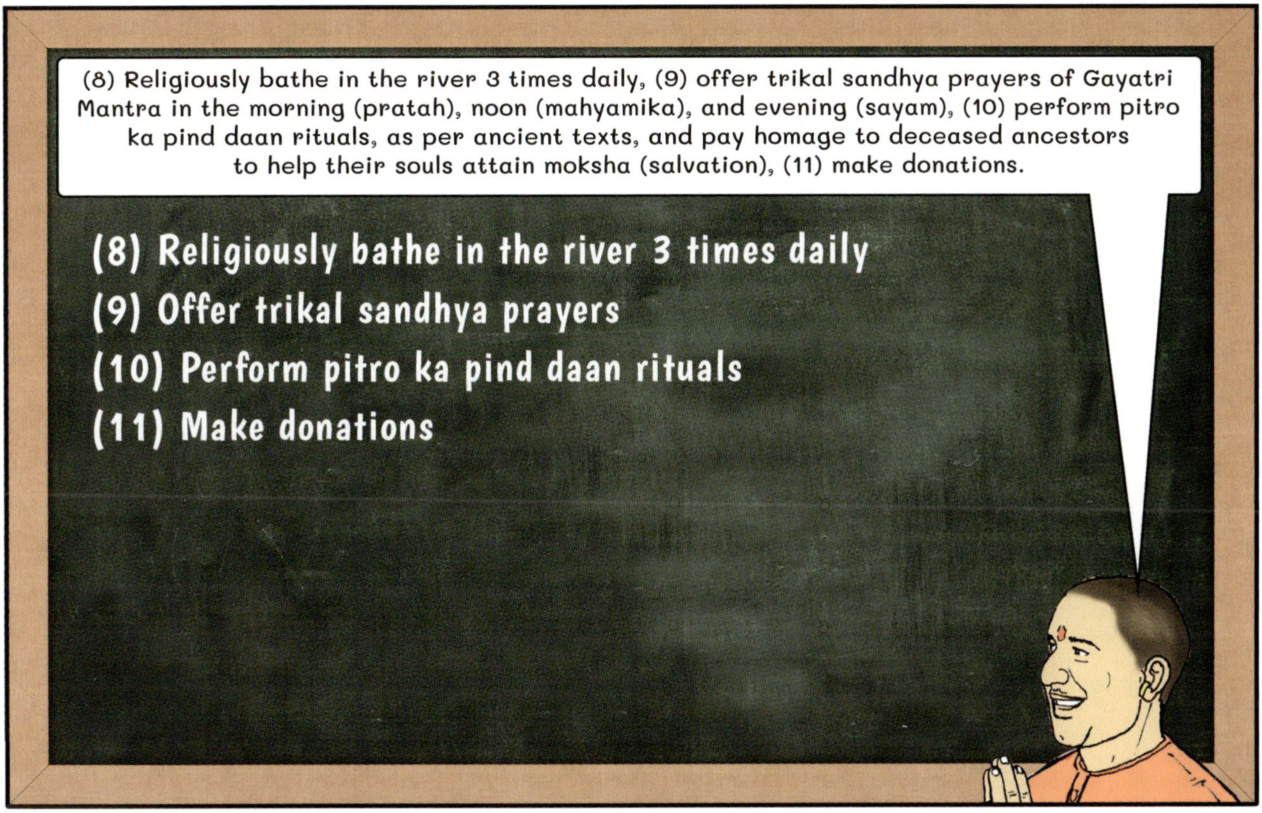
(8) Religiously bathe in the river 3 times daily, (9) offer trikal sandhya prayers of Gayatri Mantra in the morning (pratah), noon (mahyamika), and evening (sayam), (10) perform pitro ka pind daan rituals, as per ancient texts, and pay homage to deceased ancestors to help their souls attain moksha (salvation), (11) make donations.
(8) Religiously bathe in the river 3 times daily
(9) Offer trikal sandhya prayers
(10) Perform pitro ka pind daan rituals
(11) Make donations

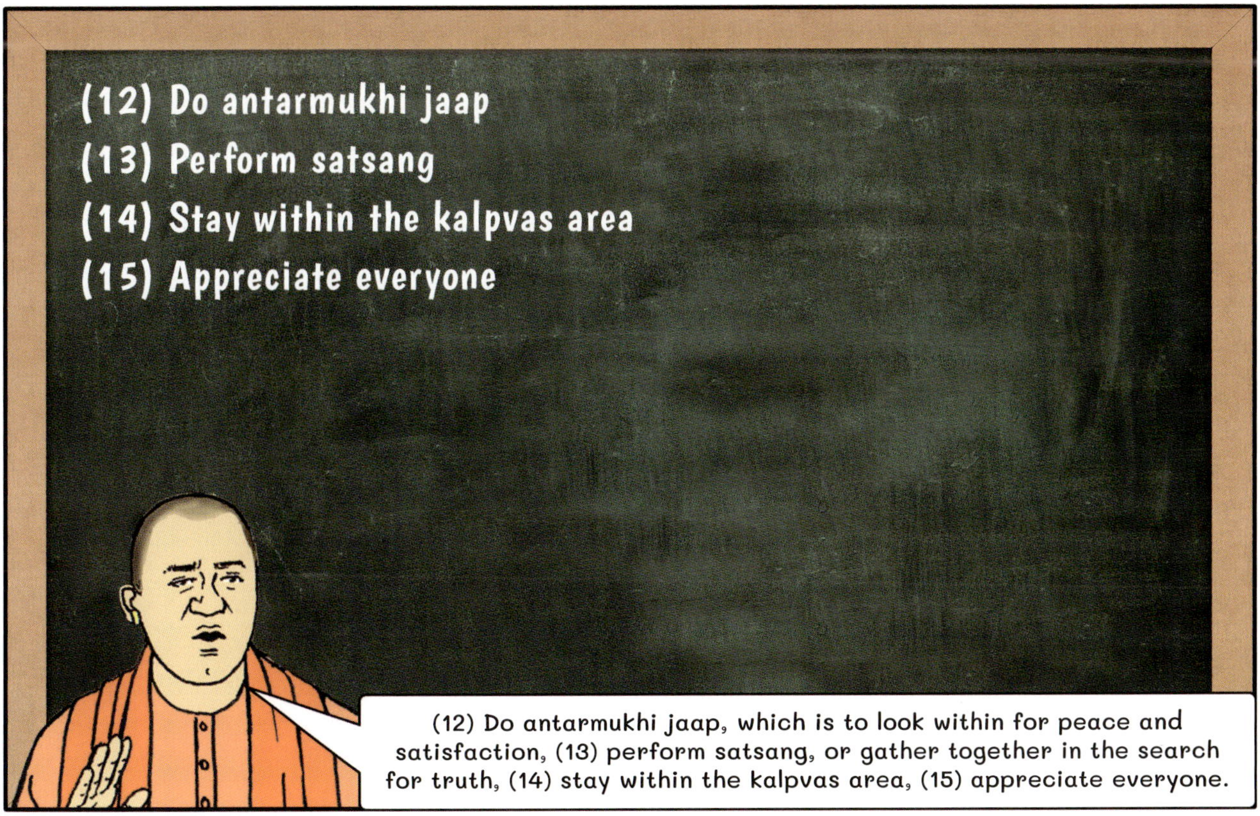
(12) Do antarmukhi jaap
(13) Perform satsang
(14) Stay within the kalpvas area
(15) Appreciate everyone
(12) Do antarmukhi jaap, which is to look within for peace and satisfaction, (13) perform satsang, or gather together in the search for truth, (14) stay within the kalpvas area, (15) appreciate everyone.

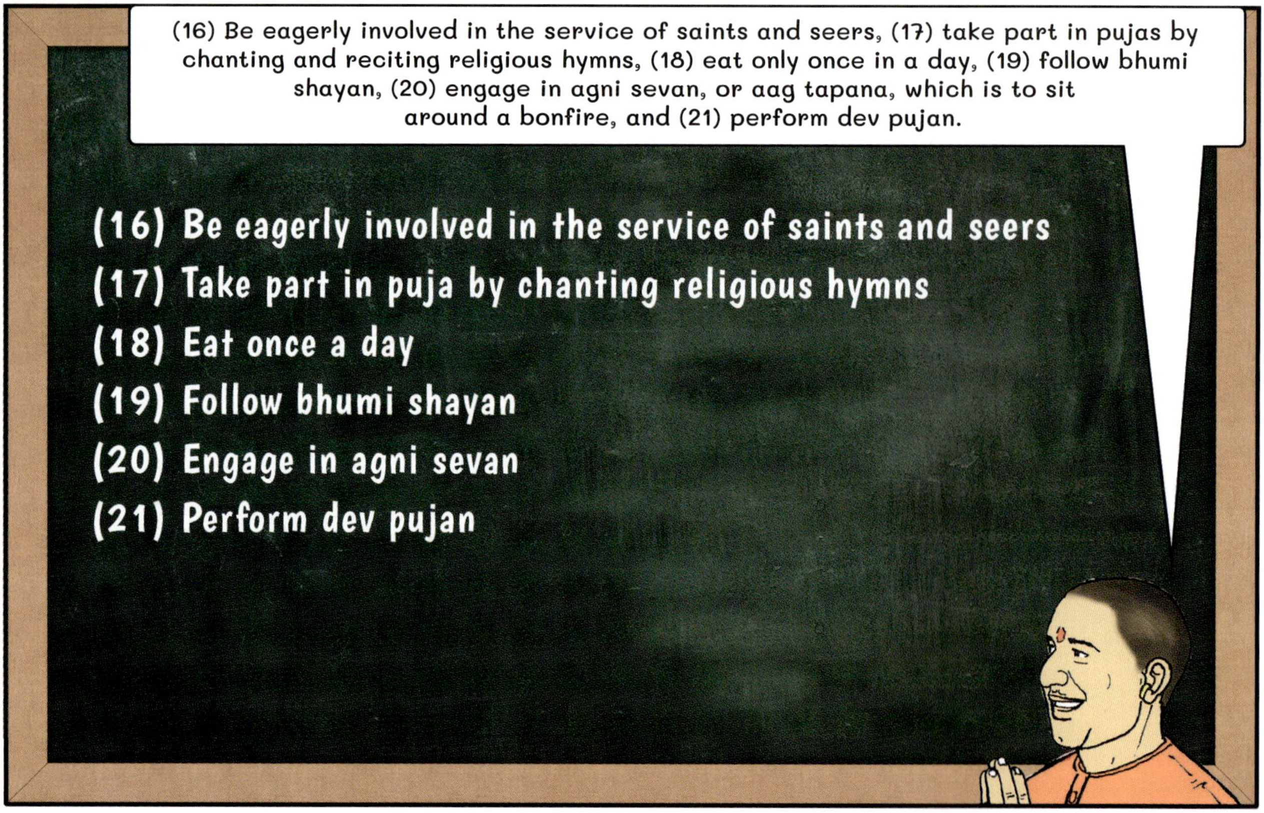
(16) Be eagerly involved in the service of saints and seers, (17) take part in pujas by chanting and reciting religious hymns, (18) eat only once in a day, (19) follow bhumi shayan, (20) engage in agni sevan, or aag tapana, which is to sit around a bonfire, and (21) perform dev pujan.
(16) Be eagerly involved in the service of saints and seers
(17) Take part in puja by chanting religious hymns
(18) Eat once a day
(19) Follow bhumi shayan
(20) Engage in agni sevan
(21) Perform dev pujan

But these are very strict and tough vows, Yogi ji?
Yes, and according to the Mahabharata, performing kalpvas for a month with these 21 guidelines is equal to offering prayers for 100 years without having a single bite of food.

MASTERCLASS
on KUMBH
Yogi ji, during colonial and Islamic rules, didn't the invaders try to stop the mela?
They did. All the invaders tried hard to create problems during the Kumbh. Under the rule of the East India Company, its officials saw Kumbh Mela as an opportunity to collect vast sums of revenue through a pilgrim tax and taxes on the trade that took place during the festival.
In fact, British officials raised the taxes to more than the average monthly income of people at the mela, causing the attendance to fall drastically! After huge resistance from the Prayagwals, they were forced to abolish the pilgrim tax,and thereafter, large numbers of devotees returned to the pilgrimage.
Who were Prayagwals, Yogi ji?
Hindu priests of Prayag were called Prayagwals.

There are accounts and records of Christian missionaries from 1814 who distributed copies of the Gospel to pilgrims and tried to convert them to Christianity.
In 1857, Colonel Neill targeted the Kumbh Mela site, shelling and attempting to destroy the areas where the Prayagwals lived.

Did we not show any resistance to these moves by the invaders?
इलाहाबाद
प्रयागराज
We certainly did. Prayagwals targeted and destroyed the mission press and churches in Allahabad (erstwhile name of Prayagraj).
But once the British regained control of the region, the Prayagwals were persecuted by the colonial officials. Some were even convicted and hanged.

Oh! So the history of Kumbh Mela has not been that smooth!
Not at all, Ganga. In fact, Kumbh Mela played an important role in the independence movement. It was a place where many people and politicians periodically gathered in large numbers to discuss ideas and plan their next moves.

In 1906, the Sanatan Dharm Sabha met at the Prayag Kumbh Mela site and resolved to start Banaras Hindu University under Madan Mohan Malaviya's leadership.
Banaras Hindu University
In 1964, Vishva Hindu Parishad was founded at the Haridwar Kumbh Mela.
Kumbh Melas have also been one of the hubs for the Ram Mandir movement over the years. The 2025 Prayag Kumbh will be the first one after the construction of the grand Ram Mandir.

Yogi ji, so this is the second Kumbh in Prayag under your leadership?
Beta, Bhagwan is the ultimate leader, we are just mediums to execute his will.

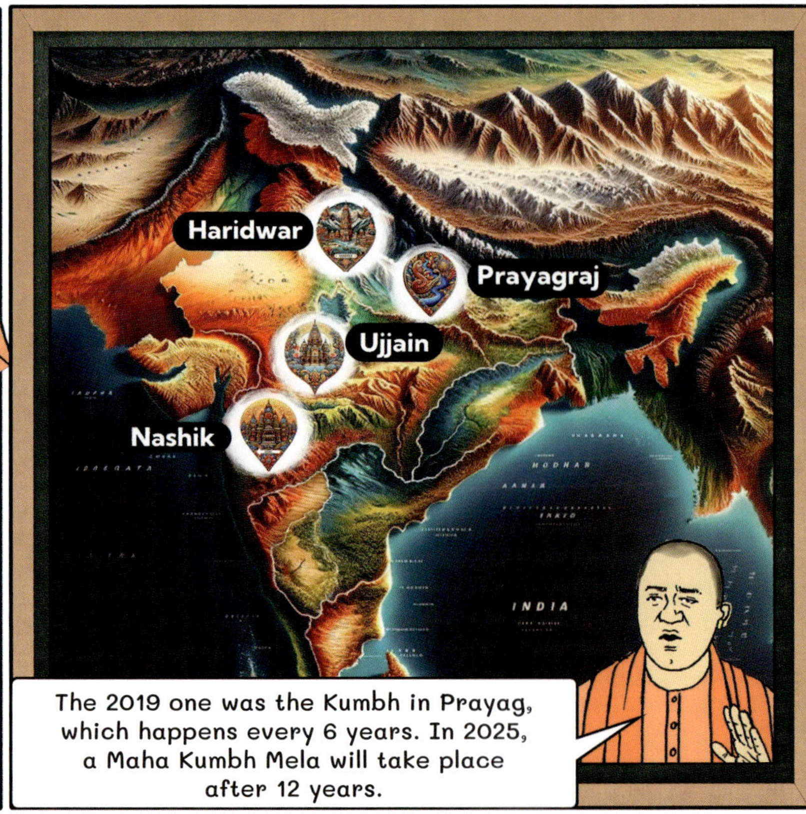
Haridwar
Prayagraj
Ujjain
Nashik
INDIA
The 2019 one was the Kumbh in Prayag, which happens every 6 years. In 2025, a Maha Kumbh Mela will take place after 12 years.

How can we know more about the 2019 Prayag Kumbh? What all happened there?

Google
https://www.kumbh.gov.in/
Maha Kumbh Mela 2025 - https://www.kumbh.gov.in
https://www.kumbh.gov.in/ - Google Search
WhatsApp Gmail Telegram Dropbox Youtube Twitter Add shortcut
You all can visit the Kumbh Mela website at www.kumbh.gov.in to learn about the 2019 and 2025 Prayag Kumbh Melas.

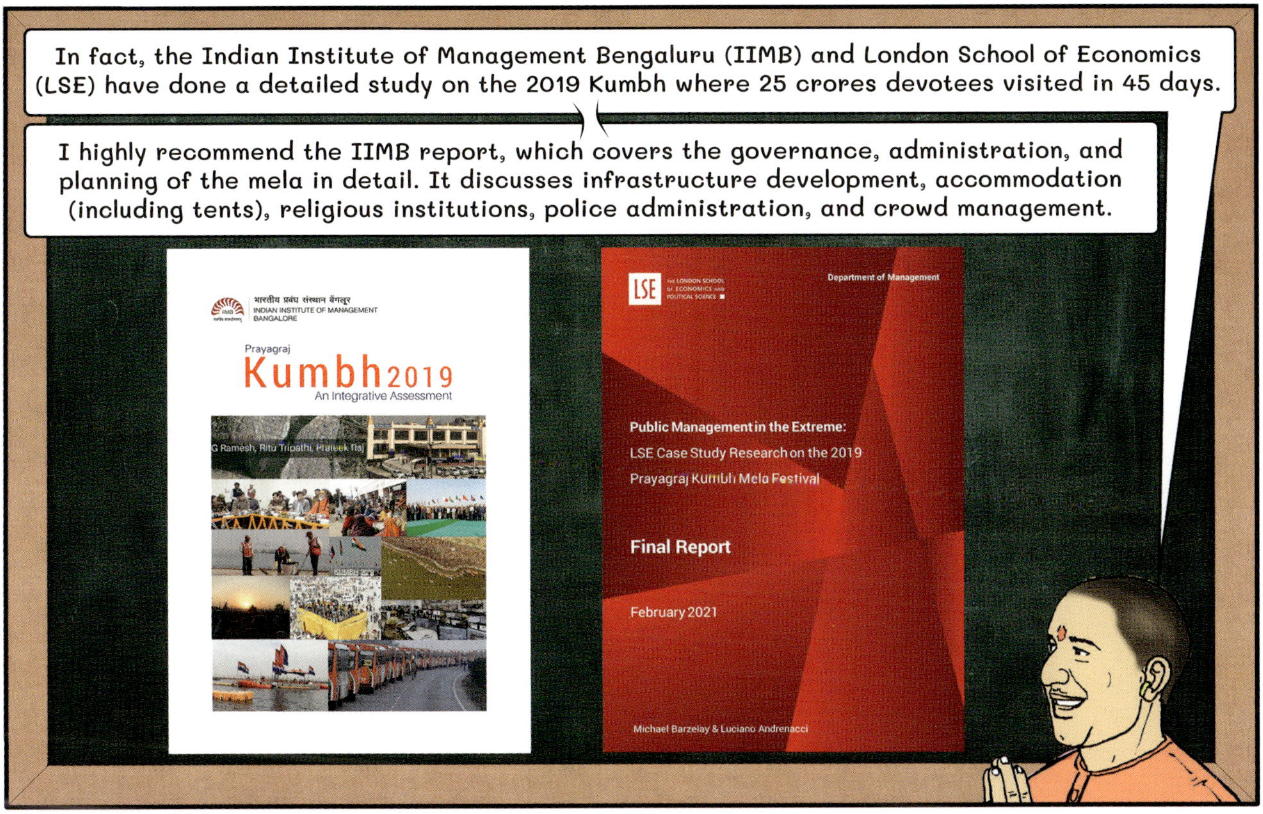
In fact, the Indian Institute of Management Bengaluru (IIMB) and London School of Economics (LSE) have done a detailed study on the 2019 Kumbh where 25 crores devotees visited in 45 days.
I highly recommend the IIMB report, which covers the governance, administration, and planning of the mela in detail. It discusses infrastructure development, accommodation (including tents), religious institutions, police administration, and crowd management.
INDIAN INSTITUTE OF MANAGEMENT BANGALORE
Prayagraj
Kumbh2019
An Integrative Assessment
G Ramesh, Ritu Tripathi, Prateek Raj
LSE
Department of Management
Public Management in the Extreme:
LSE Case Study Research on the 2019 Prayagraj Kumbh Mela Festival
Final Report
February 2021
Michael Barzelay & Luciano Andrenacci

It also touches on disaster prevention, cleanliness and hygiene, healthcare management, the lost-and-found system, transport infrastructure, logistics, vendor and procurement, as well as communications, information technology, tourism, and the culture and aesthetics of the 2019 Kumbh Mela.

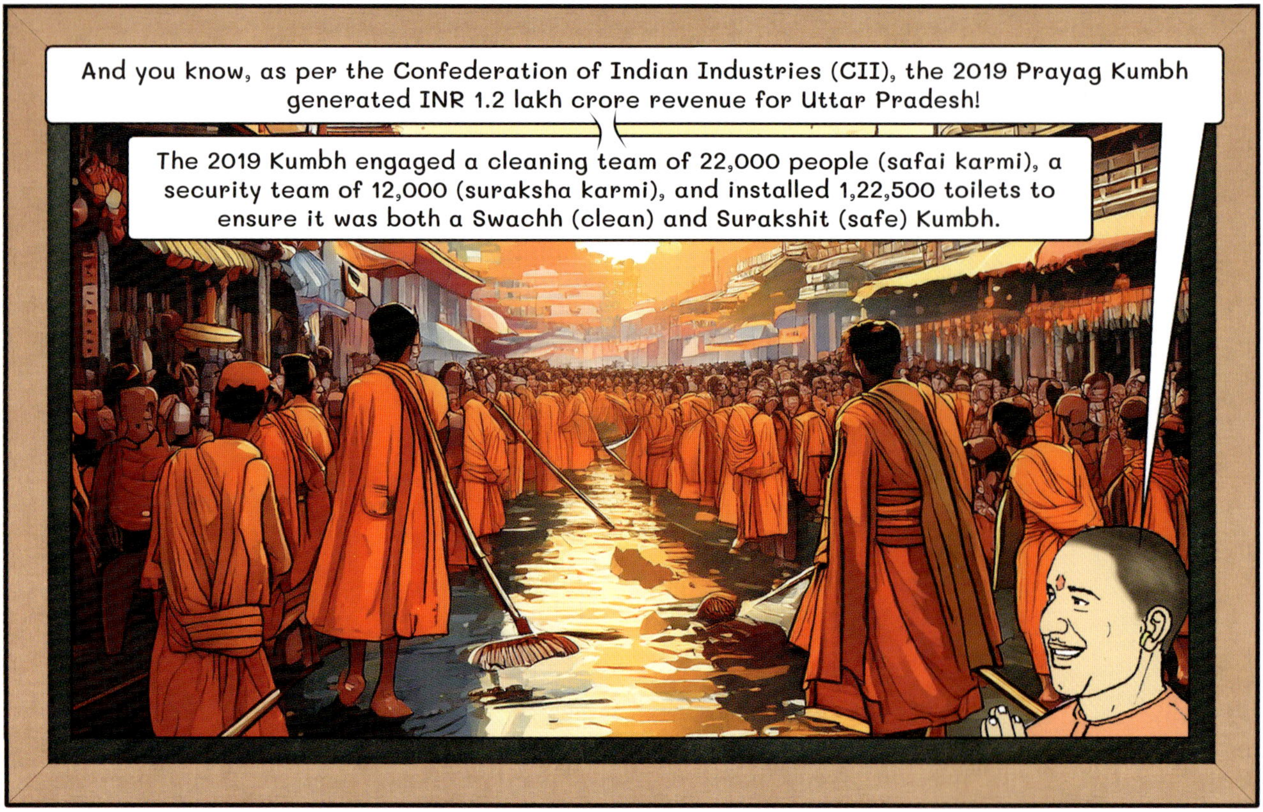
And you know, as per the Confederation of Indian Industries (CII), the 2019 Prayag Kumbh generated INR 1.2 lakh crore revenue for Uttar Pradesh!
The 2019 Kumbh engaged a cleaning team of 22,000 people (safai karmi), a security team of 12,000 (suraksha karmi), and installed 1,22,500 toilets to ensure it was both a Swachh (clean) and Surakshit (safe) Kumbh.

In fact, our PM Modi cleaned the feet of safai karmis at Prayag Kumbh 2019 as a mark of respect of their massive effort to deliver a swachh Kumbh.

So, what are the new arrangements for the 2025 Kumbh, Yogi ji?
In 2019, the mela area was 3,200 ha, and now in 2025, it has been substantially increased to 4,000 ha. So, all the facilities, will also be augmented by 25—30% over the 2019 Kumbh numbers.

Now that you all know the Puranic history of Kumbha Mela, its astrological significance, and its modern-day relevance, you all are the brand ambassadors of the Prayag Kumbh 2025!
॥सर्वसिद्धिप्रदः कुम्भः॥
महाकुम्भ प्रयागराज
2025

Yogi ji, thank you for spending so much time with the children and educating them.
MASTERCLASS
on KUMBH
Thanks to all the students for asking such intelligent and insightful questions.

GAMES & PUZZLES

Quiz Time: Let's review some facts about Kumbh Mela

1. **What does the word "Kumbh" mean in Sanskrit?**
   a) Holy River
   b) Pot
   c) Pilgrimage
   d) Festival

2. **Which Indian text is associated with the origin of Kumbh Mela?**
   a) Mahabharata
   b) Ramayana
   c) Bhagavata Purana
   d) Vishnu Purana

3. **Purna Kumbh Mela occurs in a cycle of how many years?**
   a) 6
   b) 12
   c) 3
   d) 10

4. **What celestial event determines the timing of Kumbh Mela?**
   a) Lunar eclipse
   b) Planetary alignment
   c) Solar eclipse
   d) Zodiac positions of the Sun, Moon, and Jupiter

5. **Which four cities host Kumbh Mela?**
   a) Haridwar, Prayagraj, Nashik, Ujjain
   b) Varanasi, Rishikesh, Mathura, Dwarka
   c) Delhi, Jaipur, Kolkata, Amritsar
   d) Chennai, Bengaluru, Hyderabad, Pune

6. **Which river is associated with Kumbh Mela in Prayagraj?**

   a) Ganga

   b) Yamuna

   c) Saraswati

   d) All of the above

7. **Why does Kumbh Mela happen in Haridwar, Prayagraj, Nashik, and Ujjain?**

   a) Bhagwan Vishnu declared the names of these 4 places

   b) Amrit was dropped at these 4 places after Samudra Manthan

   c) Adi Shankaracharya declared the name of these 4 places

   d) None of the above

8. **What is the significance of the nectar (amrit) in Kumbh Mela?**

   a) It is offered to the gods

   b) It grants immortality

   c) It purifies sins

   d) It is used for rituals

9. **Which king is credited with starting the modern version of Kumbh Mela?**

   a) Harshvardhan

   b) Ashoka

   c) Shivaji

   d) Chandragupta Maurya

10. **The earliest record of Kumbh Mela was made by which foreign traveller?**

    a) FaHien

    b) Xuanzang

    c) Ibn Battuta

    d) Megasthenes

11. **Along which river does the Haridwar Kumbh Mela take place?**

    a) Ganga
    b) Yamuna
    c) Saraswati
    d) Godavari

12. **Which river is associated with Nashik's Kumbh Mela?**

    a) Narmada
    b) Godavari
    c) Tapi
    d) Krishna

13. **Where does the Ujjain Kumbh Mela take place?**

    a) Ganga
    b) Shipra
    c) Chambal
    d) Betwa

14. **Name the confluence of rivers in Prayagraj.**

    a) Panch Prayag
    b) Sangam
    c) Ganga Sagar
    d) Triveni

15. **Which of the following cities is NOT associated with Kumbh Mela?**

    a) Haridwar
    b) Varanasi
    c) Ujjain
    d) Nashik

16. What is the main ritual performed during Kumbh Mela?

a) Fasting
b) Meditation
c) Holy dip in the river
d) Yagna (fire ritual)

17. Which sect is prominently involved in Kumbh Mela?

a) Shaivites
b) Vaishnavites
c) Naga sadhus
d) All of the above

18. What is the title given to the special bathing days during Kumbh Mela?

a) Ganga Jayanti
b) Makar Sankranti
c) Shahi Snan
d) Prakash Parv

19. What is the reference to the Kumbh Mela in Valmiki Ramayana?

a) Dashrath narrates the Kumbh story to Kaushalya
b) Rishi Vishwamitra narrates the Samudra Manthan story to Rama and Laxmana
c) Jambavan narrates the Kumbh story to his army
d) None of the above

20. What is the purpose of the holy dip at Kumbh Mela?

a) To achieve moksha
b) To cleanse sins
c) To purify the soul
d) All of the above

21. What marks the beginning of a Kumbh Mela?

a) Aarti

b) Religious procession

c) Hoisting of the flag by akharas

d) Astrological calculations

22. What is the interval between Ardh Kumbh Melas?

a) 3 years

b) 6 years

c) 9 years

d) 12 years

23. What is Maha Kumbh Mela?

a) A festival held annually

b) A special Kumbh Mela held every 144 years

c) A grand version held every 12 years

d) A fair for saints only

24. Who are the first participants in Shahi Snan?

a) Common pilgrims

b) Naga sadhus

c) Priests

d) Monks

25. Which Hindu god is central to Kumbh Mela rituals?

a) Lord Shiva

b) Lord Vishnu

c) Lord Brahma

d) All of the above

26. Which Indian prime minister inaugurated the 2019 Prayagraj Kumbh Mela?

a) Manmohan Singh
b) Narendra Modi
c) Atal Bihari Vajpayee
d) Rajiv Gandhi

27. Which UNESCO designation does Kumbh Mela hold?

a) World Heritage Site
b) Intangible Cultural Heritage
c) Cultural Festival of the Year
d) Global Religious Event

28. Approximately how many pilgrims visited Kumbh Mela in Prayagraj in 2019?

a) 10 crores
b) 5 crores
c) 15 crores
d) 25 crores

29. What does Purna Kumbh signify?

a) Full Moon
b) A complete cycle of 12 years
c) Complete purification
d) End of rituals

30. Who was the chief minister of UP during the 2019 Prayag Kumbh?

a) Akhilesh Yadav
b) Yogi Adityanath
c) Kalyan Singh
d) Kumari Mayawati

Crossword

Across

4. Crores of devotees take a dip at the ____________ during Prayag Kumbh.

5. Purna Kumbh Mela comes every ________ years.

7. __________ Sagar was churned during the Samudra Manthan.

11. King ______________ made Kumbh Mela widely recognized across geographies.

14. ________________ reinforced Kumbh Mela for philosophical discourses and debates among the Hindu saints.

15. ___________ river is associated with Nashik's Kumbh Mela.

Down

1. ____________ the famous Chinese traveler also documented about the Kumbh Mela in detail.

2. ___________ mountain was used as the churning stick for the Samudra Manthan.

3. Kumbh means a_______.

4. Ujjain Kumbh happens by the banks of the ________ river.

6. ____________ Purana details about the Samudra Manthan.

8. Many householders practice strict guidelines of ____________ during Kumbh.

9. ____________, Prayagraj, Nashik, and Ujjain are four cities where Kumbh Mela is celebrated.

10. Prayag Kumbh happens in the__________ month as per the Hindu calendar.

Spot 5 Differences

Spot 5 Differences

Word Search #1

Find the 4 places where Kumbh Mela is celebrated.

U	E	B	K	O	E	D	U	H	D	D
W	U	G	N	L	X	R	C	A	F	A
J	S	T	Z	R	A	M	S	R	P	D
A	Y	Q	F	P	Y	X	F	I	S	M
R	G	Z	H	T	W	R	K	D	X	M
G	K	X	H	W	N	V	G	W	T	U
A	I	J	J	Q	U	I	S	A	U	K
Y	H	A	S	A	J	A	A	R	R	R
A	S	U	N	B	S	Z	L	J	D	B
R	A	X	O	J	C	A	R	H	J	D
P	N	F	Y	Q	H	C	T	Z	W	U

HARIDWAR | UJJAIN | PRAYAGRAJ | NASHIK

Word Search #2

Find the 5 rivers associated with Kumbh Mela in different cities.

D	O	C	I	A	A	L	Y	C	D	L
L	S	A	R	A	S	V	A	T	I	L
V	T	Y	B	N	O	X	S	N	G	M
Q	S	L	A	X	F	H	M	I	U	G
L	Y	G	S	M	I	R	R	G	H	W
U	W	O	A	P	U	A	H	X	W	L
M	O	A	R	N	V	N	H	U	J	E
G	F	A	R	A	G	Z	A	X	K	R
Z	G	O	D	A	L	A	O	V	R	G
A	P	O	D	G	A	Q	S	V	Z	S
J	G	X	H	U	T	E	H	I	L	C

GANGA | GODAVARI | SARASWATI | SHIPRA | YAMUNA

Word Search #3

Find the names of the 6 akharas visiting Kumbh Mela.

M	O	V	T	O	T	V	S	D	Q	V	D	I
X	Y	Y	V	A	C	G	O	C	V	Z	M	T
N	I	R	M	O	H	I	W	T	O	B	A	R
C	H	R	A	B	M	A	G	I	D	H	H	R
J	S	Y	D	P	X	T	O	B	T	E	A	G
O	U	Z	M	O	L	X	U	P	W	V	N	A
O	Q	Z	R	L	F	V	X	N	Z	G	I	U
V	C	R	Z	Q	Z	J	A	Q	A	R	R	E
P	Y	K	T	F	P	W	C	T	G	B	V	R
W	C	A	S	I	N	A	V	R	I	N	A	H
F	S	C	J	U	N	A	L	N	S	F	N	F
N	I	R	A	N	J	A	N	I	V	H	I	Z
D	H	S	J	D	O	K	D	F	D	Z	Y	W

NIRVANI | DIGAMBAR | NIRMOHI | JUNA | NIRANJANI | MAHANIRVANI

Word Search #4

Find the names of the 6 ratnas that emerged from Samudra Manthan.

K	S	P	A	Q	C	A	A	X	T	Z	M	H
G	W	B	I	M	X	M	Y	I	U	U	G	Y
E	X	A	J	E	R	T	B	I	C	C	Q	J
Z	D	U	D	N	Y	I	L	N	O	L	J	Z
O	R	J	R	W	D	T	T	O	K	S	F	B
Z	C	L	K	H	A	L	A	H	A	L	A	I
F	P	A	N	C	H	A	J	A	N	Y	A	R
D	O	Z	G	Z	F	W	H	R	O	T	R	X
M	A	A	I	R	A	V	A	T	A	U	K	S
I	D	H	A	N	V	A	N	T	A	R	I	S
R	H	V	Y	X	F	P	M	K	X	O	L	T
Z	N	K	A	M	A	D	H	E	N	U	E	M
Q	I	W	X	H	S	Z	E	E	V	B	Z	H

AMRIT | PANCHAJANYA | HALAHALA | AIRAVATA | DHANVANTARI | KAMADHENU

Word Search #5

Find the 6 important elements attached to Samudra Manthan.

G	T	M	I	R	F	M	L	A	B
I	P	A	L	F	Q	E	O	X	H
G	P	N	K	B	R	Y	I	B	C
V	K	D	U	D	Y	A	I	U	B
N	F	A	R	E	M	K	M	S	K
M	S	R	M	I	U	R	A	S	A
M	A	A	A	S	U	R	H	A	W
P	V	E	A	P	U	I	V	G	H
W	E	V	Y	S	R	Q	U	B	Z
C	D	S	A	E	L	S	Y	Z	I

ASURAS | KSHIR | DEVAS | KURMA | MANDARA | VASUKI

Colour the Picture #1

Colour the Picture #2

Colour the Picture #3

Colour the Picture #4

Colour the Picture #5

ANSWER
KEY

Quiz

1 (b) Pot	7 (b) Amrit was dropped at these 4 places after Samudra Manthan	13 (b) Shipra	19 (b) Rishi Vishwamitra narrates the Samudra Manthan story to Rama and Laxmana	25 (b) Lord Vishnu
2 (d) Vishnu Purana	8 (b) It grants immortality	14 (b) Sangam	20 (d) All of the above	26 (b) Narendra Modi
3 (b) 12	9 (a) Harshvardhan	15 (b) Varanasi	21 (c) Hoisting of the flag by akharas	27 (b) Intangible Cultural Heritage
4 (d) Zodiac positions of the Sun, Moon, and Jupiter	10 (b) Xuanzang	16 (c) Holy dip in the river	22 (b) 6 years	28 (d) 25 crores
5 (a) Haridwar, Prayagraj, Nashik, Ujjain	11 (a) Ganga	17 (d) All of the above	23 (b) A special Kumbh Mela held every 144 years	29 (b) A complete cycle of 12 years
6 (d) All of the above	12 (b) Godavari	18 (c) Shahi Snan	24 (b) Naga sadhus	30 (b) Yogi Adityanath

Crossword

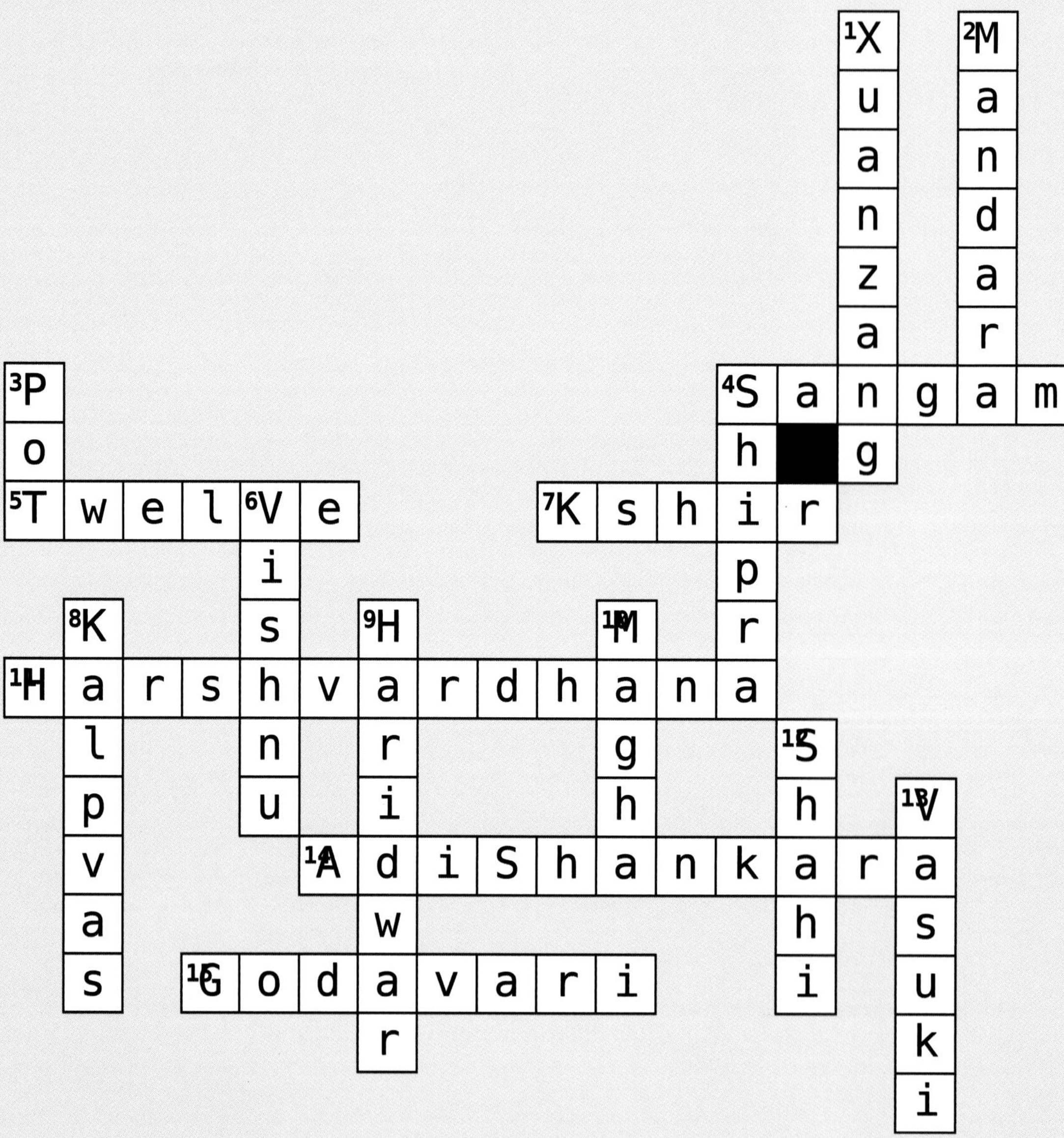
1 Xuanzang
2 Mandar
3 Pot
4 Sangam
4 Shipra
5 Twelve
6 Vishnu
7 Kshir
8 Kalpvas
9 Haridwar
10 Magh
11 Harshvardhana
12 Shahi
13 Vasuki
14 AdiShankara
15 Godavari

Spot the Differences

Word Search

Word Search #1

U	E	B	K	O	E	D	U	H	D	D
W	U	G	N	L	X	R	C	A	F	A
J	S	T	Z	R	A	M	S	R	P	D
A	Y	Q	F	P	Y	X	F	I	S	M
R	G	Z	H	T	W	R	K	D	X	M
G	K	X	H	W	N	V	G	W	T	U
A	I	J	J	Q	U	I	S	A	U	K
Y	H	A	S	A	J	A	A	R	R	R
A	S	U	N	B	S	Z	L	J	D	B
R	A	X	O	J	C	A	R	H	J	D
P	N	F	Y	Q	H	C	T	Z	W	U

Word Search #2

D	O	C	I	A	A	L	Y	C	D	L
L	S	A	R	A	S	W	A	T	I	L
V	T	Y	B	N	O	X	S	N	G	M
Q	S	L	A	X	F	H	M	I	U	G
L	Y	G	S	M	I	R	R	G	H	W
U	W	O	A	P	U	A	H	X	W	L
M	O	A	R	N	V	N	H	U	J	E
G	F	A	R	A	G	Z	A	X	K	R
Z	G	O	D	A	L	A	O	V	R	G
A	P	O	D	G	A	Q	S	V	Z	S
J	G	X	H	U	T	E	H	I	L	C

Word Search #3

M	O	V	T	O	T	V	S	D	Q	V	D	I
X	Y	Y	V	A	C	G	O	C	V	Z	M	T
N	I	R	M	O	H	I	W	T	O	B	A	R
C	H	R	A	B	M	A	G	I	D	H	H	R
J	S	Y	D	P	X	T	O	B	T	E	A	G
O	U	Z	M	O	L	X	U	P	W	V	N	A
O	Q	Z	R	L	F	V	X	N	Z	G	I	U
V	C	R	Z	Q	Z	J	A	Q	A	R	R	E
P	Y	K	T	F	P	W	C	T	G	B	V	R
W	C	A	S	I	N	A	V	R	I	N	A	H
F	S	C	J	U	N	A	L	N	S	F	N	F
N	I	R	A	N	J	A	N	I	V	H	I	Z
D	H	S	J	D	O	K	D	F	D	Z	Y	W

Word Search #4

K	S	P	A	Q	C	A	A	X	T	Z	M	H
G	W	B	I	M	X	M	Y	I	U	U	G	Y
E	X	A	J	E	R	T	B	I	C	C	Q	J
Z	D	U	D	N	Y	I	L	N	O	L	J	Z
O	R	J	R	W	D	T	T	O	K	S	F	B
Z	C	L	K	H	A	L	A	H	A	L	A	I
F	P	A	N	C	H	A	J	A	N	Y	A	R
D	O	Z	G	Z	F	W	H	R	O	T	R	X
M	A	A	I	R	A	V	A	T	A	U	K	S
I	D	H	A	N	V	A	N	T	A	R	I	S
R	H	V	Y	X	F	P	M	K	X	O	L	T
Z	N	K	A	M	A	D	H	E	N	U	E	M
Q	I	W	X	H	S	Z	E	E	V	B	Z	H

Word Search #5

G	T	M	I	R	F	M	L	A	B
I	P	A	L	F	Q	E	O	X	H
G	P	N	K	B	R	Y	I	B	C
V	K	D	U	D	Y	A	I	U	B
N	F	A	R	E	M	K	M	S	K
M	S	R	M	I	U	R	A	S	A
M	A	A	A	S	U	R	H	A	W
P	V	E	A	P	U	I	V	G	H
W	E	V	Y	S	R	Q	U	B	Z
C	D	S	A	E	L	S	Y	Z	I

About the Author

Shantanu Gupta is an author, TEDx speaker, TV panellist, and the founder of The Ramayana School. He is also a part-time faculty member at Hindu University of America and a professor at Rashtram School of Public Policy, Rishihood University. He is the first to introduce political comic books with his two graphic novels *101 Reasons Why I Will Vote for Modi* and *Ajay to Yogi Adityanath*.

His book *The Monk Who Became Chief Minister*, a biography of Yogi Adityanath, is listed as the 'Most Memorable Nonfiction Books of 2017' by Amazon India, spawning a sequel, *The Monk Who Transformed Uttar Pradesh*. His book *Bharatiya Janata Party: Past, Present and Future* has been translated into multiple Indian languages.

Shantanu has done more than 5,000 TV debates with leading channels such as India Today, CNN News18, Times Now, Republic TV, Aaj Tak, Zee News, India TV, etc. He has written opinion pieces for *The Indian Express, The Hindu, Hindustan Times, The Times of India, Dainik Jagran, Swarajya,* and OpIndia.

Shantanu is a fellow of the University of Oxford's Chevening Gurukul Fellowship. He has an engineering degree from GB Pant University (India), management degree from XLRI, Jamshedpur (India), and a master's in policy and politics from Institute of Development Studies, University of Sussex (United Kingdom). Shantanu has worked for a decade as a process and management consultant in many cities in India, Switzerland, Cyprus, Hungry, and Israel. He has represented India in many international conferences on economy and policy in Germany, Malaysia, and Sri Lanka, and worked with think tanks such as Centre for Civil Society and non-profits such as UNICEF, Naandi Foundation, and National Independent Schools Alliance.

Notes

Notes

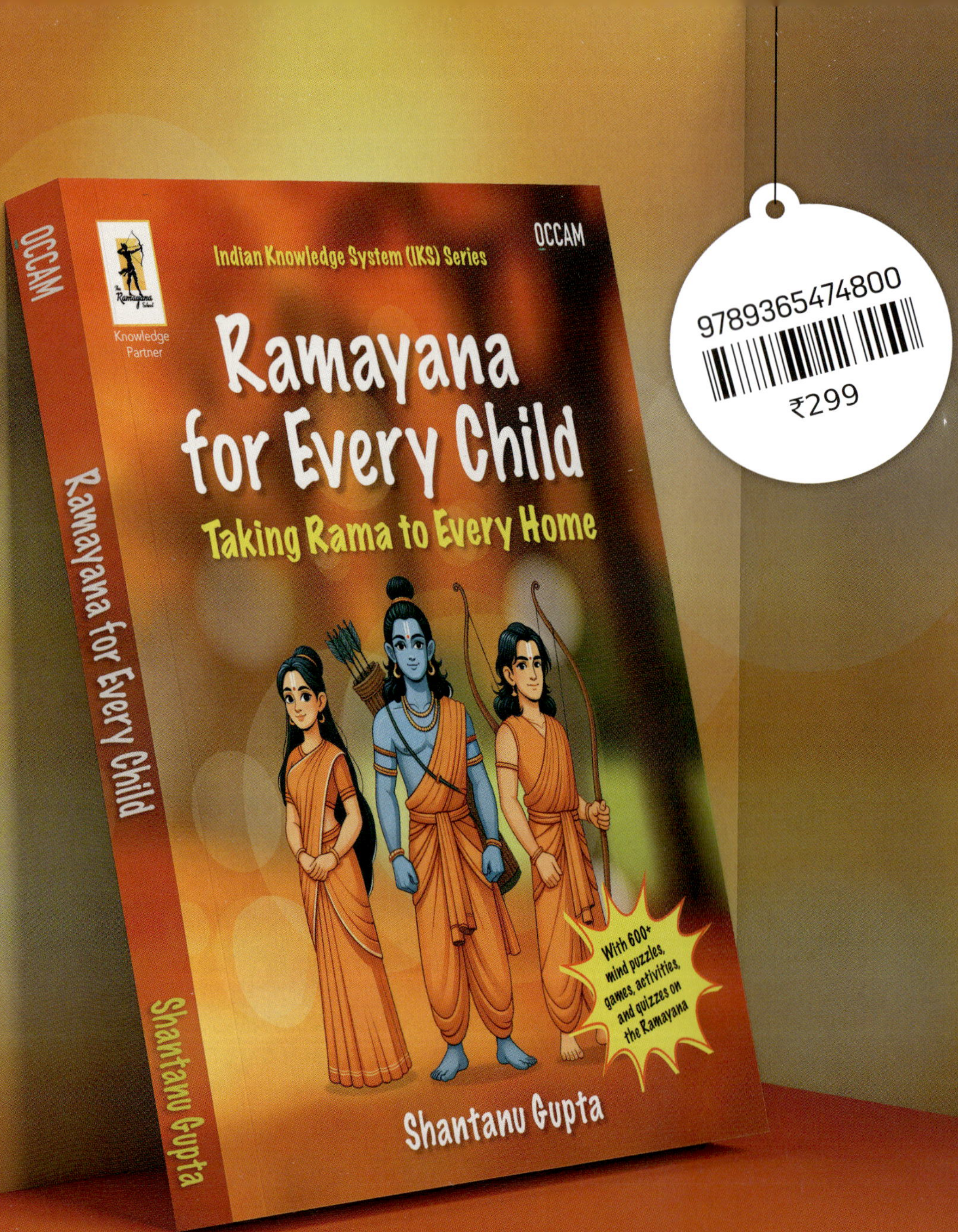

"Bhagwan Ram is within all of us."

Prime Minister Narendra Modi